HOW WE GOT THE BIBLE

MADE EASY

How We Got the Bible Made Easy

Published by Rose Publishing
An imprint of Tyndale House Ministries
Carol Stream, Illinois
rose-publishing.com

ISBN 978-1-62862-824-1

The *Made Easy* series is a collection of concise, pocket-sized books that summarize key biblical teachings and provide clear, user-friendly explanations to common questions about the Christian faith. Find more *Made Easy* books at www.hendricksonrose.com.

Contributing author: Len Woods

Printed in China
December 2024, 3rd printing

CONTENTS

"For everything that was written in the past was written to teach us, so that through the endurance taught in the Scriptures and the encouragement they provide we might have hope."

ROMANS 15:4

It's been called the Word of God, the Sacred Scriptures, Holy Writ, and the Good Book. While some people revere the Bible, others revile it. Some want to get copies of the Bible into the hands of all people everywhere; others would gladly rid the world of this ancient collection of Jewish and Christian teachings. Where did this controversial book even come from? How did we get it?

In this concise guide, we'll survey the history of the Bible from the ancient origins of biblical writings to the most popular Bible translations in the present day. In the next few pages, we'll tackle questions like these:

- Where did the Bible come from? Who wrote it—and when?
- Who decided which writings would be included in the Bible—and which ones would be left out?
- What's a *testament*? And why does the Bible have an "old" one and a "new" one?
- Where did all those different Bible translations come from?
- Why should we trust that the Bible is accurate in what is says?

For readers who want to ponder these subjects further—or for those who want to read through this book with a few others—we've included some discussion questions at the end.

But first, let's begin with five big questions about the Bible.

FIVE BIG QUESTIONS ABOUT THE BIBLE

What Exactly Is the Bible?

MANY THINK THE BIBLE IS A THOUSAND-PLUS pages of religious restrictions and requirements. Not true.

Instead, let's try looking at it like this. Imagine rooting around in your great-grandfather's basement. Buried in the corner next to an old gramophone is a big, overstuffed briefcase. Your heart races—maybe it's full of gold, jewels, or money! Actually, it's even better than that. Within that leather portfolio you discover a treasure trove of old family documents: love letters and postcards from World War II, news clippings of major events, and tattered, blurry snapshots of relatives you didn't even know you had! Inside, you find birth and baptismal records, property deeds, marriage licenses, death certificates, and family genealogies. From

that dusty satchel, you retrieve poems from someone's old journal, three or four outdated maps, plus a few vacation souvenirs. At the bottom of the briefcase, you even come across some old sheet music, a few "secret" family recipes, and folded-up building plans for your granddad's place, the old family homestead. What you have stumbled upon, of course, is a family history. All those individual documents and artifacts combine to tell the unique story of a specific family—yours.

In a real sense, this is what the Bible is. It's a written history of the people of God. Within the leather covers of that big family Bible (or your cool modern study Bible) is an assortment of ancient texts by dozens of authors—kings, prophets, scribes, followers of Jesus, and others. These writings were composed over a period of some twelve to sixteen centuries! (For comparison's sake, Charles Dickens wrote *A Christmas Carol* in only six weeks.) After these biblical documents were written, they were copied, circulated, gathered together, guarded, recopied, and passed down through the generations.

Even though it's technically an anthology of sixty-six smaller books, the Bible tells one epic story. Like our "briefcase in the basement" example, the assorted books within the Bible include a variety of material. Among the first thirty-nine books of the Bible—what Christians call the Old Testament—are lengthy narratives of Israel's distant history and detailed records of moral and ceremonial law. Other Old Testament books consist of poetic or wisdom literature, and others are prophetic in nature. The final twenty-seven books of the Bible—called the New Testament—include narratives of the life of Jesus and a history of the first three or more decades of the Christian movement. These historical records are followed by a number of letters (some not much longer than a postcard) written to specific churches and individuals. The New Testament ends with the famous book of Revelation, an eye-popping book of wild imagery and heavenly visions of what is and what's to come.

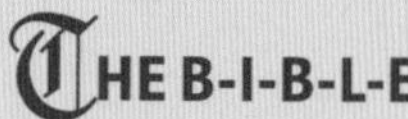

Our English word *Bible* comes from the Greek word *biblion*, which means "scroll" or "book." A similar term, *biblos*, was used to refer to the papyrus material shipped from the ancient port city of Byblos. Many biblical manuscripts were written on papyrus. The plural of *biblion* is *biblia*, and the term came to refer to a collection of holy writings or sacred scriptures. Jerome, a scholar in the fourth century who translated the Bible into Latin, called the books of the Bible "the Divine Library."

Two Testaments, One Story

The word *testament* means "agreement" or "covenant." When someone dies, he or she leaves behind a last will and testament. This document spells out certain legally binding promises. In this sense, the Old Testament is a record of how the covenant and promises that God made with the Jewish patriarch Abraham unfolded (see Genesis 12) up until about four centuries before the time of Jesus.

What Christians refer to as "the Old Testament," Jews call "the Tanakh." *Tanakh* actually comes from an acronym (TNK) formed by the first letters of the three recognized sections of the Hebrew Bible: the Torah (the five books of Moses), the Nevi'im (the eight books of the Prophets), and the Ketuvim (the eleven books of writings). Christians subdivide these same twenty-four books into thirty-nine books and put them in a different order. It's the same material, just presented in a different arrangement.

Christians further see the New Testament as a record of how Jesus of Nazareth revealed himself to be the fully human and fully divine Son of God. The New Testament documents present Jesus as the Messiah, the great king and deliverer foretold by the Jewish prophets in the Tanakh. They see his life, death and resurrection as God's way of inaugurating a new covenant between God and all humanity (both Jews and non-Jews).

The Bible, then, is a single story—the written record of God's efforts to seek and save humanity. It has one consistent, overriding message: we humans will remain restless until we stop running from God, turn to him in faith, and find rest in the love and forgiveness of Christ Jesus. Observant readers marvel at the many ways the Old Testament foreshadows the events of the New Testament, at how it ingeniously points to the coming of Jesus. Christians believe the New Testament completes the story of the Old Testament.

What Tools Did Biblical Writers Use?

Writers today tap away on computer keyboards and store their work in the digital cloud. The ancients used slightly more primitive tools. Many settled for writing on stone, wet clay, even pottery. The biblical authors used reed pens and ink made from a concoction of gum (resin) and soot. They wrote on parchment and papyrus.

Parchment is animal skin from sheep, cattle, or goats that has been scraped, stretched thin, dried, and then cut into sheets. Fine, top-of-the-line parchment (usually made from calf skin) is called vellum. Parchment sheets were stitched together to form long rolls, called scrolls. Beginning in the late first or early second century and continuing through the Middle Ages, parchment sheets were also bound into primitive books called codices (singular: codex).

While the Old Testament writers and copyists preferred parchment, New Testament documents were mostly written and copied on papyrus. The papyrus plant grows in marshy, wetland regions, like the delta of the Nile River in Egypt. Its stems were cut into thin strips and laid side by side. One layer was laid at right angles to and

Artisan making papyrus paper

on top of another, then pressed tightly and dried. The resulting material was a fairly durable paper that could be made into a scroll or a codex.

Of the two materials, parchment was by far the more expensive to produce. A really large codex could require the skins of perhaps two hundred animals! On the plus side, parchment was much more enduring than papyrus. Occasionally the writing on a parchment was scraped off, and a scribe would write a new document on top of the old, "erased" text. Such a manuscript is called a *palimpsest*, from a Greek phrase meaning "rubbed smooth again."

WHAT'S A CODEX?

A codex is a bound volume resembling a primitive book. It consists of sheets folded and stitched together, sometimes with a cover. Christians began using codices instead of scrolls around the early second century. Unlike a scroll, a codex allowed writing on both sides of the parchment or papyrus.

Parchment codex

What Makes the Bible Different from Other Books?

The Bible makes a spectacular claim about itself: that it has a divine origin. Some 3,800 times it features the phrases, "God said" or "Thus says the Lord." The Bible presents itself as the actual Word of God!

In the New Testament, the apostle Paul, a devout Jew and a follower of Jesus, wrote, "All Scripture is inspired by God and profitable for teaching, for reproof, for correction, for training in righteousness" (2 Timothy 3:16 NASB).

Scripture means "writing" and, in this Bible verse, refers to the collected writings that the people of God regard as having a divine origin.

Inspired literally means that the biblical writings are "God-breathed"—*not* that they're "feel-good" or "goose-bump inducing." Inspiration isn't that God took some mere human ideas and added a little heavenly "oomph" to them; it's that God worked in and through the various human authors of Scripture—supernaturally prompting and guiding them—so that using their own unique personalities and vocabularies and writing styles, they composed and recorded, without any errors, the exact messages that God wanted to reveal to people.

Sometimes, God told the Bible writers the precise words to say (for example, Jeremiah 1:9). In these instances, the process of inspiration was almost like dictation. Other times, God used the unique minds, vocabularies, cultures, and experiences of these human authors to convey his message through them. This accounts for the sharp stylistic differences between the Bible books.

The apostle Peter, a Jewish Christian, writes in the New Testament, "Above all, you must understand that no prophecy of Scripture came about by the prophet's own interpretation of things. For prophecy never had its origin in the human will, but prophets, though human, spoke from God as they were carried along by the Holy Spirit" (2 Peter 1:20–21). (Note how, later in the letter, Peter also recognized the apostle Paul's writings as coming from God; 2 Peter 3:15.) The Greek verb translated in this verse as "carried along" was also used to describe a ship being driven by a strong wind. For example, in Acts 27:15–17, there is an account of sailors trying to navigate in a storm, but they were unable to make the ship go

Apostle Peter

where they wanted it to go. Ultimately, they had to let the strong wind take them wherever it would blow. The sailors were active and involved, but the wind ultimately determined the ship's destination. So it was in the writing of Holy Scripture. Both God and humans were involved in its production, but the end result was what God wanted. He is the ultimate author. He directed the writing and guaranteed the accuracy of it. There was definite human involvement, but no human agenda.

Where Can We See the Original Bible Writings?

We can't.

We don't have the original writings of Scripture. The psalms of David, the letters of Paul—all those original documents, plus the writings of Moses, Isaiah and all the others, are long gone, lost in the mists of history. No one should be surprised by this fact. Documents deteriorate. If you've ever stood in the National Archives building in Washington D. C. and looked through

the dim light at the Declaration of Independence, you know how faded and worn it is—and it's not even two hundred and fifty years old! (And for the last sixty-five years, it's been carefully protected, first in a bronze case filled with helium—and now in a titanium case filled with inert argon gas; it's even kept under special bulletproof glass designed to filter out all harmful light.)

Parchment and papyrus crumble, especially when they are exposed to the elements and handled frequently. This is why ancient documents had to be copied and recopied constantly. This explains why we have *thousands* of scrolls, scroll fragments, and codex leaves (two-sided pages).

Textual Criticism

Textual criticism is the study of all available ancient copies of texts in order to reconstruct the wording of the original (or at least, the earliest) documents. In a real sense, textual critics today are a lot like the lab geniuses we see on TV shows like *C.S.I.*, except rather than investigating crimes, they are doing painstaking scientific analysis of very old manuscripts. They compare these ancient documents, date them, and figure out the order in which they were produced. When they have a bunch of manuscript fragments, they assemble them back together like puzzle pieces. By comparing different styles of lettering, they can group manuscripts in "families" or "schools." And by (no joke!) doing DNA testing on various parchment documents, they can tell which ones came from the same flock or even the same animal skin! Thanks to state-of-the-art, high-resolution, 3D scanning technology, these researchers can now read the all-but-invisible writing on ancient fragments, even documents that have turned black with age or been charred in fire. They now use computer algorithms to virtually unroll scrolls that are too fragile to physically unroll.

Multispectral imaging showing palimpsest fragments in infrared (left) and ultraviolet (right) parts of the spectrum

The point is, modern textual criticism isn't mystical guesswork. It's real science. Think of it as documentary genealogy or literary detective work. By it, scholars can trace the origin and history—the family tree—of various scrolls and codices.

With all these copies, and thanks to the science of textual criticism, we know that the Jewish scribes who copied the Scriptures by hand—long before the days of printing presses and copy machines—were obsessed with accuracy and precision. Their aim was to fiercely guard and preserve the wording of the original biblical writers. The discovery of the Dead Sea Scrolls in 1947 confirmed how carefully and reliably the scribes worked to preserve the Old Testament writings. One of the Dead Sea Scrolls is a scroll of Isaiah, dating to 125 BC. This scroll was found to be almost identical to other Isaiah manuscripts that had been copied a thousand years later!

This isn't to say that there aren't any variations between the biblical manuscripts. There are. Manuscripts sometimes have a different word order, a spelling variant, a missing phrase—the kinds of normal mistakes you'd expect when copying anything by hand, over and over. Bible scholars are honest about these variations and other discrepancies. Many Bibles include marginal notes pointing out these differences. Princeton's Bruce Metzger, perhaps the preeminent New Testament scholar of the twentieth century, concluded that after being copied for centuries and centuries, only forty of the 20,000 lines of the New

WHAT IS INERRANCY?

Inerrancy is the belief that the original writings of Scripture—because of their divine origin—were "God-breathed" without error. To the extent that our modern translations accurately represent the original text, we have a trustworthy Bible.

Scroll of Isaiah

Testament are debatable. He noted that none of these variances affects the basic tenets of the Christian faith.[1] They don't call into question what we believe about God or about how he works in the world. Therefore, we can trust our modern-day Bibles.

Why Are There So Many Bible Translations?

The Old Testament was written primarily in Hebrew, with a few parts of the books of Daniel and Ezra written in Aramaic.

What's Aramaic? Glad you asked! Aramaic was similar to Hebrew and used in Babylon. When the Jewish people were exiled to Babylonian territories in the sixth century BC, many Jews began speaking Aramaic almost exclusively. In fact, after they were allowed to return to their homeland in Judea, Aramaic was still so popular among the people that the Hebrew Scriptures were translated into Aramaic so that everyone could understand God's Word. These translations were later called the Targums, a word

11th century Hebrew Bible with Targum

that means "to translate" or "to explain." By the time of Jesus in the first century, most Jews, including Jesus, spoke Aramaic.

The New Testament, however, was written in Koine Greek (*koine* means "common"). This was because by the first century, Greek was the popular trade language used across the vast Roman Empire. The Greek translation of the Hebrew Bible (or Old Testament) became known as the Septuagint (more on that later).

Some of the earliest translations of the Bible were in Latin (Rome), Coptic (Egypt), and Syriac (Syria). Jerome's Latin translation in AD 405, called the Vulgate, became the official Bible of the western church for many centuries.

As Christianity spread all over the world, the need arose to translate the story of God—the Bible—into the languages of these different populations. And so . . .

- By AD 200, portions of the Bible had been translated into 7 languages.
- By 500, 13 languages.
- By 900, 17 languages.
- By 1400, 28 languages.
- By 1800, 57 languages.
- By 1900, 537 languages.

Today, some 3,384 languages have at least a portion of the Bible, and 1,548 languages have a full New Testament or more. All together, humans speak almost 6,500 languages (though almost a third of those are spoken by very small numbers of people). Clearly, more Bible translation work is needed.[2]

Because of constant changes in language and culture, advances in scholarship, and the Bible's long-running popularity, to date there have been around 450 translations of the Bible into English alone!

There is little doubt that the Bible is the world's best-selling and most widely distributed book. A survey by the Bible Society concluded that around 2.5 billion copies were printed between 1815 and 1975, but more recent estimates put the number at more than 5 billion.[3]

Now that you have a kind of big picture overview of the Bible, let's look more closely at how the first and oldest part of the Bible—the Old Testament—came to be.

THAT SAYING IS FROM THE BIBLE?

Thanks to the immense popularity of the King James Bible in the first three hundred years of American life, daily conversations and culture are peppered with biblical phrases and expressions like:

"Go the extra mile" (Matthew 5:41).

"There's nothing new under the sun" (Ecclesiastes 1:9).

"Like mother, like daughter" (Ezekiel 16:44).

"An eye for an eye" (Exodus 21:24).

"A thorn in the flesh" (2 Corinthians 12:7).

"Salt of the earth" (Matthew 5:13).

"The powers that be" (Romans 13:1).

"You reap what you sow" (Galatians 6:7).

"At their wit's end" (Psalm 107:27).

"A voice crying in the wilderness" (Matthew 3:3).

"Wolves in sheep's clothing" (Matthew 7:15).

HOW WE GOT THE OLD TESTAMENT

Where Did the First Books of the Bible Come From?

TODAY, GOD'S WORD IS AS CLOSE AS YOUR smartphone or a good Wi-Fi connection. Did you know that as of 2020, the popular Bible App® has been downloaded on more than 400 million unique devices, giving Bible readers translations or paraphrases of the Bible in some 1,350 languages?[4] Today, 66 percent of the world's population can access a full Bible in their own language on the internet.[5] Such instant availability makes it hard for us to grasp that there once was a time when Bible didn't exist.

To see how the Bible came to be, we have to go back around 3,400 years. Here's the story in brief: The Jewish people, recently freed from Egyptian slavery, gathered at the base of Mount Sinai while Moses, their leader, went to the summit to meet with Almighty God. It was there that the Israelites entered into a covenant with God. It was then that God revealed his will—his plans and promises—for his people. The second book of the Bible, Exodus, describes the scene. It says that Moses "wrote down everything that the LORD had said" (Exodus 24:4). A short time later, God gave Moses two tablets of stone said to be "inscribed by the finger of God" (Exodus 31:18). For Christians and Jews, this encounter is viewed as the beginning of the composition of the Torah, the first five books of the Bible—also known as the Pentateuch, the Law, or the five books of Moses.

For the next eight or so centuries, Israel wandered in the desert south of Canaan; settled in the promised land; lived under a series of judges and kings; constantly battled their enemies; gradually turned away from God; watched their nation disintegrate; went into exile; and then returned from captivity to rebuild their land. During this long period, the Lord moved on the hearts of prophets, kings, scribes, and unknown individuals to write down stories, lessons, and principles that he wanted preserved for posterity. He had these assorted writers chronicle historical events, compose poems, songs, wise sayings, and also record chilling and thrilling prophecies.

In time, all these writings became what Christians know as the Old Testament:

- **FIVE BOOKS OF LAW**
  Genesis through Deuteronomy
- **TWELVE HISTORICAL BOOKS**
  Joshua through Ruth
- **FIVE POETIC/WISDOM BOOKS**
  Job through Song of Songs (Song of Solomon)
- **SEVENTEEN PROPHETIC BOOKS**
  Isaiah through Malachi

There are many details we don't know about the actual "creation" of these thirty-nine books: how in each instance this mysterious divine and human collaborative process worked; who specifically wrote each and every Old Testament book; when precisely each of these writings first appeared as ink on parchment.

But there is much we do know. We know that ancient Jewish culture was an oral culture. They carefully memorized, constantly repeated, and faithfully handed down the stories of God's marvelous acts in history. We know too that the ancient Jewish people were literate; they could read and write. We know they kept written records (Exodus 17:14; Numbers 21:14; Deuteronomy 10:1–4; 27:8; 31:19; 2 Chronicles 12:15). Given all these oral traditions and careful records, at any point, a person guided by the Spirit could have sat down and faithfully recorded whatever God wanted revealed. We know that occasionally the prophets were explicitly commanded by God to put his messages in writing (Jeremiah 36:2).

The writings of the Old Testament were copied and recopied many times over the centuries. So who copied all those crumbling scrolls in ancient Israel? Answer: An educated group of people known as scribes (the Hebrew word is *soferim*, which means "people who can write"). As with Israel's priests, if you were born into a scribal family, you were almost certainly going to become a scribe; it was the family business (1 Chronicles 2:55). Not every document that the scribes copied was "spiritual" (1 Kings 4:3; 1 Chronicles 27:32), but when scribes copied the Torah, they followed strict rules. They took a ritual bath called a

A sofer completing the book of Esther

mikveh. They never worked with implements of steel or iron, since those materials were used in weapons of war.[6] They were extremely careful. In fact, Torah scrolls that were found to have even one missing letter were prohibited from being used in public worship. (The widely accepted number of letters of the Torah is 304,805.)

WHAT DOES *CANON* MEAN?

That word *canon* is actually a Greek word that means "reed," "standard," or "measuring stick." Books considered canonical are books that measure up to the standard of being divinely inspired. It's important to point out that this quality of canonicity is not something humans confer on or decide about a document; it's something that humans recognize in a document.

The years after the exile—roughly from 500 BC to the time of Jesus in the first century AD—was an era when many scholars think the books of the Hebrew Bible were gathered and arranged into a widely accepted canon of Scripture. By the time of Jesus, the Hebrew Bible was frequently called "the Law, the Prophets, and the Writings," "the Law, the Prophets, and Psalms," or simply, "the Law and the Prophets" (Luke 16:16; 24:44). The apostle Paul referred to the Hebrew Scriptures as "the old covenant" (2 Corinthians 3:14).

Books of the Old Testament

BOOK	AUTHOR	DATE WRITTEN	TYPE OF WRITING
JOB	Unknown	Unknown	Poetry/ Wisdom
GENESIS	Moses	1446–1406 BC	Narrative/Law
EXODUS	Moses	1446–1406 BC	Narrative/Law
LEVITICUS	Moses	1446–1406 BC	Narrative/Law
NUMBERS	Moses	1446–1406 BC	Narrative/Law
DEUTERONOMY	Moses	1446–1406 BC	Narrative/Law
JOSHUA	Unknown (possibly Joshua or Samuel)	1300s BC	Narrative
JUDGES	Unknown (possibly Samuel)	1350–1000 BC	Narrative
RUTH	Unknown (possibly Samuel)	1350-1000 BC	Narrative
1 AND 2 SAMUEL	Unknown	1100-931 BC	Narrative
PSALMS	David (73 psalms) Asaph (12 psalms) Sons of Korah (11 psalms) Other writers	1000–450 BC	Song/Poetry
PROVERBS	Solomon and others	900s–700s BC	Poetry/ Wisdom
ECCLESIASTES	Unknown (possibly Solomon)	900s or 500s BC	Wisdom
SONG OF SONGS	Possibly Solomon and/or later writers	900s or 500s BC	Song/Poetry
JONAH	Jonah	783–753 BC	Narrative/ Prophecy

BOOK	AUTHOR	DATE WRITTEN	TYPE OF WRITING
AMOS	Amos	760–753 BC	Prophecy
HOSEA	Hosea	752–722 BC	Prophecy
ISAIAH	Isaiah	740–681 BC	Prophecy
MICAH	Micah	738–698 BC	Prophecy
NAHUM	Nahum	663–612 BC	Prophecy
ZEPHANIAH	Zephaniah	641–628 BC	Prophecy
JEREMIAH	Jeremiah	626–582 BC	Prophecy
HABAKKUK	Habakkuk	609–598 BC	Prophecy
DANIEL	Daniel	605–535 BC	Narrative/ Prophecy
EZEKIEL	Ezekiel	593–571 BC	Prophecy
LAMENTATIONS	Jeremiah	586 BC	Lament
OBADIAH	Obadiah	586 BC	Prophecy
1 AND 2 KINGS	Unknown	561–539 BC	Narrative
HAGGAI	Haggai	520 BC	Prophecy
ZECHARIAH	Zechariah	520–518 BC	Prophecy
1 AND 2 CHRONICLES	Unknown (possibly Ezra)	450–400 BC	Narrative
EZRA	Ezra	400s BC	Narrative
NEHEMIAH	Ezra	400s BC	Narrative
ESTHER	Unknown	400s BC	Narrative
MALACHI	Malachi	400s BC	Prophecy
JOEL	Joel	Unknown (possibly 400s BC)	Prophecy

All dates are approximate. Books are listed in the order in which they're believed to have been written, not the order they appear within the biblical narrative.

Can God's Word Be in a "Pagan" Language?

With advances in technology, translating a document today from one language to another is a snap—in the words of the popular commercial, "so easy a caveman can do it." This wasn't the case 2,300 years ago when a major Bible translation project was badly needed. Here's the story:

Shortly after the Jews had put the Babylonian captivity in their rearview mirror, they came under the thumb of another great world empire. In the fourth century BC, the Greeks, led by the brash Alexander the Great, conquered much of the Near East. What was young Alexander's ambition? He wanted the whole world—Jews included—to embrace Greek culture, philosophical ideas, and religion. Alexander got his way; it wasn't long before almost everyone was scrambling to learn Greek.

Portrait of Alexander the Great on an ancient Greek gold coin

Within the Jewish community, this cultural pressure created enormous tension. As it became increasingly important to know Greek to conduct business, fewer and fewer Jews across the Mediterranean were speaking

Hebrew and Aramaic. The need for the Hebrew Scriptures to be translated into Greek became apparent. Others, however, were appalled by this suggestion; the very idea that a pagan language like Greek would be used to translate the Word of God! Nevertheless, the project was undertaken, and it was completed around 255 BC.

Septuagint fragment from the Dead Sea Scrolls, (1st century BC)

This translation of the Hebrew Bible into Greek came to be known as the Septuagint and was often abbreviated as the Roman numeral LXX, meaning "seventy." *Septuaginta* also means "seventy" and refers to the legend that seventy-two Jewish scholars completed this translation in only seventy-two days. Apparently, not wanting to call their translation the *Septuaginta Duo*—Latin for "seventy-two"—they went with the closest round number.

Because of this new translation, Jews with no knowledge of Hebrew could read God's Word for themselves. Non-Jews were also able to read the Word of God for the first time! And here's a little-known fact: Most of those Old Testament quotations that we find in the New Testament (which was written in Greek) came from the Septuagint.

Why Do Some Bibles Have "Extra" Books?

Flip open a Catholic Bible and you'll quickly notice that there's a different list of books than in the Bibles at the Baptist church down the road. Instead of thirty-nine Old Testament book, you'll count forty-six. If it's an Eastern Orthodox Bible, you'll count even more books. So why do some Bibles have these "extra" books?

St. Jerome in His Study
by Domenico Ghirlandaio

Evidence derived from first century Jewish writers—like the historian Josephus—suggests that the Hebrew Bible did not originally contain these books. However, the books were included in the Septuagint, the Greek version of the Hebrew Bible. In AD 382, the scholar Jerome was commissioned by Pope Damasus to translate the Bible into Latin, the accepted language of the Roman Empire. Jerome was working from the Old Testament Hebrew and Aramaic texts and had serious misgivings about including those other Greek books from the Septuagint. Reluctantly, he added the books in his new Bible translation, called the Vulgate, but with some disclaimers. Jerome labeled these extra books *apocryphal*, from a Greek word that means "hidden" or "unclear." Others preferred to call them deuterocanonical, which means "second canon" or "added to the canon." In later editions of the Vulgate, Jerome's disclaimers disappeared.

In 1546 at the famous Council of Trent, the Roman Catholic Church declared these books to be Holy Scripture. The Synod of Jerusalem in 1672, an Eastern Orthodox Church Council, affirmed the books to be "genuine parts of Scripture."[7] Most Protestant Christian Bibles today do not include the apocryphal books.

The Council of Trent by Pasquale Cati

Books of the Apocrypha

ROMAN CATHOLIC	EASTERN ORTHODOX
Tobit	Tobit
Judith	Judith
1 Maccabees	1 Maccabees
2 Maccabees	2 Maccabees
	3 Maccabees
Wisdom of Solomon	Wisdom of Solomon
Sirach (aka Ecclesiasticus)	Sirach (aka Ecclesiasticus)
Baruch (includes the Letter of Jeremiah)	Baruch (includes the Letter of Jeremiah)
Additions to Esther	Additions to Esther
Additions to Daniel (includes the Prayer of Azariah and Song of the Three Holy Children), Susanna, Bel and the Dragon)	Additions to Daniel (includes the Prayer of Azariah and Song of the Three Holy Children), Susanna, Bel and the Dragon)
	1 Esdras
	The Prayer of Manasseh
	Psalm 151

Why Was a Lost Goat Such a Big Deal?

It's a story right out of Hollywood. A teenaged goatherd searching for a stray goat throws a rock into a cave opening near the Dead Sea hoping to hear a scared bleat. What he hears instead is the sound of breaking pottery. Scrambling up and into the darkness, the young man finds several large jars containing ancient parchments. The precise details of this story—exactly who, what, when, where, why, and how—are debated. What is not disputed is the fact that this supposed lost goat precipitated the greatest literary and archaeological find of the twentieth century.

Since 1946, in twelve different caves in the Judean desert near the Dead Sea, Bedouin treasure hunters and international teams of scholars have discovered hundreds of ancient biblical documents and thousands of other manuscript fragments. The oldest scrolls date to about 300 BC; the most recent ones may have been written around AD 40. These documents, known collectively as the Dead Sea Scrolls, contain portions of every Old

Hebrew scroll found near the Dead Sea

Testament book except Esther. Though they are not the original Old Testament documents, they are the oldest copies in existence.

Many scholars believe these documents belonged to a strict Jewish religious sect who lived in the desert at Qumran, separate from the rest of society. Known as the Essenes, these Jews were dedicated to moral and religious purity. They shared property, rigorously observed the Sabbath, followed special diets, and took ritual baths. Among the writings found at Qumran are copies of the Hebrew Scriptures, rules about holiness within the group, commentaries on Scripture, marriage contracts, calendars, and even horoscopes.

Qumran caves

According to Jewish tradition, old, tattered, faded biblical documents were never burned or destroyed. After they were copied, they were gathered and stored in a special place called a *genizah,* and eventually buried in a reverent way. The scrolls found near Qumran, however, weren't being buried or retired; they were hidden away to be protected. In AD 68, the Roman army was on the march, quelling a Jewish uprising in the region. It seems that in the same way that we store our important documents "in the cloud," the members of the Qumran community were trying to preserve their precious manuscripts "in the caves." And there the scrolls remained for almost two thousand years.

The Dead Sea Scrolls are extremely important for demonstrating how accurately the Old Testament writings were copied down through the centuries. How so? Before we found them, our oldest copies of the Old Testament dated back only about a thousand years, to around AD 1000. The writings found at Qumran pushed that date back by another thousand years or more. When we compare the later manuscript copies to the Dead Sea Scrolls produced a thousand years earlier, the text is remarkably close. For example, the text of the Isaiah scroll found at Qumran produced about 125 BC is nearly identical to the Isaiah text in the Ben Asher Codex produced in AD 1008. This shows that the text of the Old Testament was carefully copied and preserved over many centuries.

Jar and cover for manuscript rolls (1st century BC)

If It's *Old,* Why Should We Keep Reading It?

If you've ever tried to read the Bible from start to finish, you know that it's easy to get bogged down quickly. Genesis is no problem; it's got those great stories of Adam and Eve, Noah's ark, the adventures of Abraham, and the up-and-down life of Joseph, the good-looking kid with the multi-colored coat. Exodus, the second book, also begins with lots of excitement—Israel's miraculous deliverance from Egypt and the parting of the Red Sea. But the final third of Exodus is a long section of laws, followed by an extended discussion of plans for the tabernacle, Israel's portable worship facility. The next book, Leviticus, is page after page of detailed instructions for the sacrifices and regulations for the priests to follow. The fourth book, Numbers, contains extensive census records (not exactly riveting reading). The fifth book, Deuteronomy (which means "second law"), is essentially Moses repeating God's law to a new generation of Israelites.

Many Bible readers, if they even make it this far, conclude, *Perhaps I'll just*

turn over to the New Testament and read some stories about Jesus.

That's a mistake. A misstep. Or at least a misunderstanding. The Old Testament is worth reading in its entirety. It is the Bible Jesus used. It's the holy book Jesus grew up reading and memorizing and meditating upon—and loving. To really understand Jesus, we have to understand his Bible.

Jesus Unrolls the Book in the Synagogue by James Tissot

When the devil tempted Jesus in the wilderness at the beginning of his ministry, Jesus beat back this diabolical attack by quoting three verses from the book of Deuteronomy (Matthew 4:1–11; Luke 4:1–13). In his teaching and even from the cross, Jesus quoted from the book of Psalms (Matthew 21:42; Mark 15:34). He routinely cited passages from Isaiah (Luke 4:17–19). You don't have to read long into the New Testament to realize that Jesus' thinking was utterly shaped by the truth of the Old Testament.

But that's not all.

In the New Testament, Luke tells a fascinating story about how, after Christ had risen from the dead, he suddenly joined a couple of his dejected followers as they trudged toward the little town of Emmaus (Luke 24:13–35). It's a strange and funny encounter for at least two reasons: first, the men didn't recognize Jesus; second, Jesus "played dumb" as the men started talking about the tumultuous weekend in Jerusalem. He listened as the men mentioned the latest rumors about the Lord's tomb being empty—and they made it clear that they weren't so sure about that story. As far as they were concerned, Jesus was dead . . . and so was his movement. Jesus had heard enough. Luke, the author of the third gospel, writes:

Mosaic of Jesus with the disciples on the road to Emmaus (Emmauskirche Church, Berlin)

> [Jesus] said to them, "How foolish you are, and how slow to believe all that the prophets have spoken! Did not the Messiah have to suffer these things and then enter his glory?" And beginning with Moses and all the Prophets, he explained to them what was said in all the Scriptures concerning himself. (Luke 24:25–27)

Shortly after that, Jesus appeared to Peter and the other disciples. When Jesus realized that they also were struggling to make sense of his death and resurrection, Luke tells us that Jesus said:

> "This is what I told you while I was still with you: Everything must be fulfilled that is written about me in the Law of Moses, the Prophets and the Psalms." Then he opened their minds so they could understand the Scriptures. (Luke 24:44–45)

Don't miss what Jesus was saying in these two extraordinary encounters. He was claiming to be the focal point of the Old Testament Scriptures! The "Law of Moses, the Prophets and the Psalms" was first-century shorthand for "all the Scriptures." We could paraphrase his words this way: *From Genesis 1:1 to Malachi 4:6, the Old Testament is all about me!*

That's why we need to read it. And why we miss out if we don't.

HOW WE GOT THE NEW TESTAMENT

What's There to See in the New Testament?

ONE OF THE MOST PROMINENT NEW Testament figures was a fisherman-turned-apostle named John. In fact, he wrote about twenty percent of the New Testament. At the beginning of his account of the life of Jesus, John introduces Jesus as "the Word" (John 1:1, 14).

Consider this: What are words for, except to communicate and to make ourselves understood? With that intriguing description, John was saying that Jesus was the living, breathing "explanation" of Almighty God (John 1:18). Jesus is the Creator's way of saying to his creatures, *This is who I am and what I'm like.* Given this introduction of Jesus as the living Word of God, we could think of the New Testament as written words about the living Word.

Apostle John

The New Testament continues and completes the story of the Old Testament by presenting Jesus as Israel's long-awaited Messiah, the world's much-needed Savior. The twenty-seven books of the New Testament describe how Jesus perfectly fulfilled the law of God and gave himself as a final and complete sacrifice for sin. Through Jesus, God has made a new covenant (a new agreement) with the world: Anyone (Jew or non-Jew) who trusts in Christ Jesus for forgiveness and new life becomes a member of God's forever family. The time for accepting God's gracious offer is now, because the New Testament also says that Jesus is coming again.

Let's explore this good news!

Before traveling to a new city, walking through a strange mall, or buying tickets to a movie, most people wonder, *What's there to see here? What can I expect to find?* In that spirit, here is a peek at what's in the twenty-seven books of the New Testament:

- **FOUR GOSPELS**

  The New Testament begins with four accounts of the life and ministry of Jesus. (The word *gospel* means "good news.") The writers were Matthew and John (apostles of Jesus) and Mark and Luke (close associates of the apostles). These gospels aren't typical biographies in the modern sense of the word. They are more like theological portraits of the life and ministry of Jesus. If we were to coin a word, we could call them *theolographies*.

- **THE BOOK OF ACTS**
  Also called "Acts of the Apostles," this book is Luke's "sequel" to his gospel. In it, he chronicles the beginning and expansion of the early church in the first thirty or so years after Jesus.

- **TWENTY-ONE EPISTLES**
  These letters were written to various churches and individual Christians. Thirteen are authored by the apostle Paul and known as the Pauline Epistles. The other eight are referred to as the General Epistles and were written by James (the brother of Jesus), Peter, John, and others.

- **THE BOOK OF REVELATION**
  This last book of the New Testament (and the Bible) is apocalyptic in nature, meaning that it envisions a great change in the world where God's kingdom is manifest. This is communicated to the apostle John (the author of Revelation) through awe-inspiring visions and symbolic imagery.

Books of the New Testament

BOOK	AUTHOR	DATE WRITTEN	TYPE OF WRITING
JAMES	James	AD 49	Letter to Jewish Christians across the Roman Empire
GALATIANS	Paul	AD 49	Letter to Christians in the region of Galatia
MARK	John Mark	AD 50s	Account (gospel) of the life of Jesus
1 THESSALONIANS	Paul	AD 50–51	Letter to Christians in Thessalonica
2 THESSALONIANS	Paul	AD 50–51	Letter to Christians in Thessalonica
1 CORINTHIANS	Paul	AD 55–56	Letter to Christians in Corinth
2 CORINTHIANS	Paul	AD 56	Letter to Christians in Corinth
ROMANS	Paul	AD 57	Letter to Christians in Rome
MATTHEW	Matthew (Levi)	AD 60s	Account (gospel) of the life of Jesus
LUKE	Luke	AD 60–62	Account (gospel) of the life of Jesus
ACTS	Luke	AD 60–62	History of the early church
EPHESIANS	Paul	AD 60–62	Letter to Christians in Ephesus
PHILIPPIANS	Paul	AD 60–62	Letter to Christians in Philippi
COLOSSIANS	Paul	AD 60–62	Letter to Christians in Colossae

BOOK	AUTHOR	DATE WRITTEN	TYPE OF WRITING
PHILEMON	Paul	AD 60–62	Letter to Philemon, a member of the church in Colossae
1 TIMOTHY	Paul	AD 62–66	Letter to Timothy, a pastor in Ephesus
1 PETER	Peter	AD 64	Letter to Christians in Asia Minor
2 PETER	Peter	AD 64	Letter to Christians in Asia Minor
TITUS	Paul	AD 64–66	Letter to Titus, a pastor in Crete
2 TIMOTHY	Paul	AD 66–67	Letter to Timothy, a pastor in Ephesus
HEBREWS	Unknown	AD 60s	Letter to Jewish Christians
JUDE	Jude	AD 60s–80s	Letter to Christians everywhere
JOHN	John	AD 85–95	Account (gospel) of the life of Jesus
1 JOHN	John	AD 85–95	Letter to Christians in Asia Minor
2 JOHN	John	AD 85–95	Letter to the "Elect Lady," which could mean the church
3 JOHN	John	AD 85–95	Letter to Gaius, a Christian in Asia Minor
REVELATION	John	AD 95	Apocalypse and letters churches in Asia Minor

Books are listed in the order in which they're believed to have been written. Dates are approximate and give a time span within which the book was written.

What Were the Languages in the New Testament Era?

Even though Aramaic was the everyday language spoken by Jews—including Jesus—in the first century, the New Testament books were written in Greek (though some scholars think there may have been an Aramaic edition of Matthew's gospel that is now lost to history).[8]

Why Greek? Because Greek was the common trade language used throughout the Mediterranean world during the time of the New Testament. Diverse people all across the Roman Empire would be able to read books and letters written in Greek.

The Lord's Prayer in Aramaic and Hebrew
(Church of the Pater Noster on the Mount of Olives, Israel)

The gospels of Matthew and Mark sometimes interrupt the Greek and quote Jesus using Aramaic words.

BIBLE VERSE	ARAMAIC TRANSLITERATION	ENGLISH TRANSLATION
MATTHEW 5:22	*Raca*	Fool
MATTHEW 27:46	*Eli, Eli, lema sabachthani*	My God, my God, why have you forsaken me?
MARK 5:41	*Talitha koum*	Little girl, I say to you, get up!
MARK 7:34	*Ephphatha*	Be opened!
MARK 14:36	*Abba*	Father

Latin was the language used by Roman officials in the time of the New Testament. This explains why, when Jesus was crucified, Pilate had the inscription "Jesus of Nazareth, the King of the Jews" written in Hebrew/Aramaic, Latin, and Greek, and posted above Christ's head (John 19:19–20). Interestingly, with this act the Roman governor was unwittingly "sharing the gospel" with the widest possible audience!

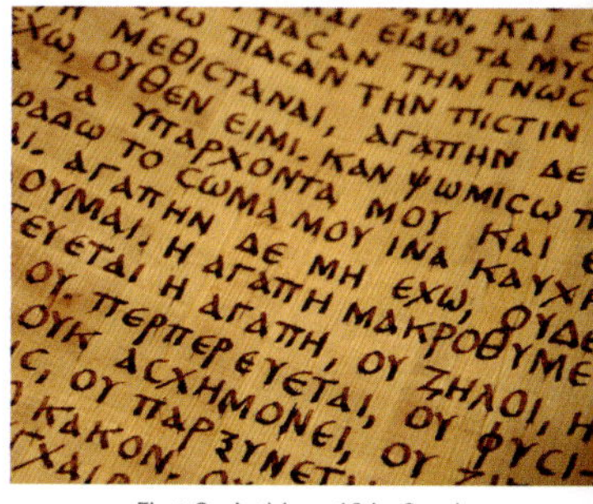

First Corinthians 13 in Greek

Why Did They Choose *Those* Twenty-Seven Books?

After Jesus rose from the dead and just before he returned to heaven, he told his followers to spread his good news of forgiveness and new life to people in Jerusalem, Judea, Samaria, and eventually to the ends of the earth (Acts 1:8). Empowered by the Holy Spirit, they did just that. The church, God's new community, was born.

As the message of Jesus spread and groups of Christ-followers began forming all over, false teachers and "make-believers" began infiltrating these congregations. They challenged the teachings of Jesus and the apostles, advocated opposing religious ideas, and caused much confusion. The apostles (and those close to them) responded with a whole body of literature in the second half of the first century—assorted documents that clarified the beliefs of "Christians," as some were calling them (Acts 11:26).

As these writings circulated among churches in Asia, Europe, and North Africa, they were copied and translated. In the second and third centuries, more writings and additional "gospels" popped up and began to circulate as well. These documents contained stories and ideas that contradicted the teaching in the gospels of Matthew, Mark, Luke, and John, and in the letters of the apostles.

Church leaders had criteria for distinguishing between divinely *inspired* works and those that were of human origin. The questions they wrestled with were along these lines:

- Is the work tied to a recognized and revered leader of the church? Writings not verifiably connected to an apostle of Christ were discounted.
- Is the work from the first century? Later works were immediately viewed with suspicion.
- Is the content of the work in agreement with the explicit teaching of Jesus and the apostles? Writings that deviated from widely accepted Christian truth were rejected.
- Has the work sparked authentic spiritual life and growth in readers far and wide?
- Does the work have an undeniable supernatural quality—a kind of holy "weightiness"?

Twenty-seven books measured up to the standard of "showing the marks of inspiration." These were regarded as canonical. Years after a number of early church leaders like Athanasius, Jerome, and Augustine had already listed these books as the New Testament canon, three separate church councils, including the Synod of Carthage in AD 397, also affirmed the books as being God's inspired word for the church.

It bears repeating: Canonicity isn't a label that a group of people bestows upon a writing; it is a quality that godly people recognize in a writing. Dr. Timothy Paul Jones explains it this way:

> No church council or bishop created the New Testament canon; instead, Christians recognized and received a canon that God created. This canon was breathed out by God as Christ-commissioned eyewitnesses and their close associates authored the books of the New Testament. A unanimous consensus emerged no later than the second century regarding the four Gospels, Acts, the letters of Paul, and at least the first letter from John. By the end of the fourth century, Christians had concluded that twenty-seven texts—the same texts found in your New Testament still today—could be traced back to apostolic eyewitnesses and their associates.[9]

2,000 YEARS OF BIBLE HISTORY (IN ABOUT 10 MINUTES)

Time Line: AD 100–Present

Here's a whirlwind tour of the key people and biggest moments in the Bible's formation, preservation, and translation from the end of the first century to today.

YEAR	EVENT
100	**John**, the last remaining of Jesus' twelve apostles, dies of natural causes around AD 100, possibly in Ephesus. He wrote five books of the New Testament, including the book of Revelation, the last book of the Bible.
170	The **Muratorian Fragment**, a copy of a document dating to around AD 170, lists all the books of the New Testament except Hebrews, James, and the epistles of Peter. This gives us a peek into which books Christians in the second century regarded as canonical.

Muratorian Fragment

180 Around AD 180, church leader **Irenaeus of Lyon** describes how the four Gospels are considered by Christians to be Scripture given by God.

Irenaeus of Lyon

286 In AD 286, the **Roman Empire** is divided into two parts. Rome becomes the capital of the West and Byzantium (Constantinople) the capital of the East.

303 Roman ruler **Diocletian** issues an edict against Christianity (AD 303). He orders church buildings to be torn down and calls for copies of Scripture to be burned.

313 A decade later, **Emperor Constantine** officially legalizes Christianity with the Edict of Milan, ending the official persecution of Christians by Roman authorities.

Emperor Constantine

325 The **Council of Nicaea** (AD 325) affirms the divinity of Jesus, effectively refuting the claims of the Gnostic gospels like *Gospel of Philip*, *Gospel of Judas*, and *Gospel of Thomas*.

300s ▶ **Codex Vaticanus** and **Codex Sinaiticus**, two of the oldest surviving Greek Bibles today, are written in the early to mid-fourth century.

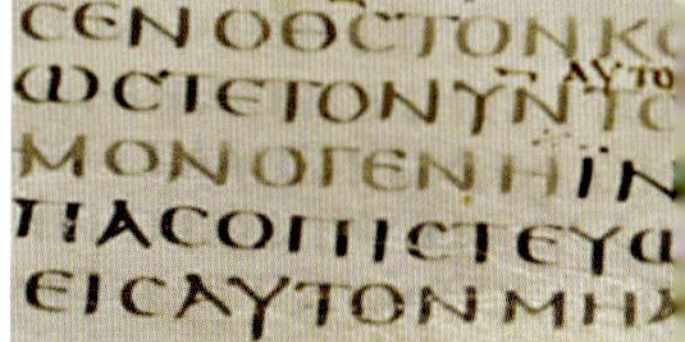

Greek lettering in Codex Sinaiticus

367 ▶ Athanasius writes his famous **Easter Letter** (AD 367), specifying the books of the Bible that Christians recognized as authoritative. He lists the twenty-seven books that we have in our New Testaments today.

382 ▶ In Rome in AD 382, a monk named Jerome begins translating the Scriptures from Greek and Hebrew into Latin. He finishes twenty-three years later. His translation becomes known as the **Latin Vulgate**, from *vulgo*, meaning "to make common, accessible" or literally "vulgar." His translation uses words the average person of his day could understand. The Latin Vulgate becomes the most popular translation of the Bible in the Western church for the next thousand years.

Saint Jerome in His Study by Antonio da Fabriano II

397 ▶ The **Synod of Carthage** (or Council of Carthage) is held in AD 397. This synod confirms the canon listed by Athanasius and used in churches in the West.

399 ▶ By the close of the fourth century, the Bible has been translated into Latin (Rome), Coptic (Egypt), and Syriac (Syria). These are some of the **earliest translations** of the Christian Bible.

400 ▶ Jewish scribes, called the **Masoretes**, work to preserve the Hebrew and Aramaic Scriptures for at least six centuries (about AD 400–1000). Since Hebrew and Aramaic have no written vowels, the Masoretes add accents and vowel markings ("vowel points") to guide readers. They keep precise statistics about how often certain words are used, differences (variants) in the manuscripts, and the number of words in each book and section of the Scriptures. The Old Testament preserved by the Masoretes is known today as the Masoretic Text. The oldest surviving complete copy of the Masoretic Text dates to AD 920.

Aleppo Codex, a Masoretic text dating to the 10th century

400s ▶ **Codex Bezae** is written during the fifth century. It is a side-by-side version of some New Testament books in both Greek and Latin.

476 ▶ The **Roman Empire** declines and eventually collapses in the west. Germanic tribes migrate into the former Roman Empire and new languages develop.

596 ▶ Christianity reaches Britain before AD 300, but Anglo-Saxon pagans drive Christian Britons into Wales (AD 450–600). In AD 596, **Augustine of Canterbury**, "the apostle to the English," renews efforts to bring the gospel to England. As Christianity spreads to the English-speaking world, multiple efforts are made to translate the Bible into **Old English**:

Augustine of Canterbury

- **Caedmon**, an illiterate monk, retells portions of Scripture in Anglo-Saxon (Old English) poetry and song (AD 676).
- **Aldhelm**, the bishop of Sherborne, is said to have translated the Psalms into Old English (AD 709).

- A monk and scholar named **Bede** creates an Old English translation of portions of the Bible from the Latin Vulgate to make the Bible accessible to pastors who can't read Latin. He dies in AD 735 while translating John's gospel; his translation is lost to history.

Alfred the Great

- **Alfred the Great**, the king of Wessex, translates the first fifty psalms into Old English (AD 871–899). He has Old Testament passages, such as the Ten Commandments, rendered into Old English and incorporated into his code of law.

- The **Lindisfarne Gospels** in the early eighth century is produced in a monastery in Northumberland (northern England). It is an illuminated (meaning, illustrated and decorated) Latin manuscript of the four gospels. Aldred, Bishop of Durham, inserts a translation in Northumbrian (a dialect of Old English) between the lines of the Latin text of the gospels (AD 950).

Folio 27r from the Lindisfarne Gospels

- **Aelfric** (AD 955–1020) turns portions of the Latin Old Testament into Old English.

Charlemagne

800 ▶ In AD 800, **Charlemagne** (a.k.a. King Charles) becomes the first Holy Roman Emperor and is crowned by the Pope, bringing sacred and secular powers together.

800 ▶ The **Pauper's Bible**, an assortment of illustrated Bibles in the Middle Ages (AD 800–1500), tells Bible stories through pictures for those who cannot read. It takes many forms, from elaborate illuminated manuscripts to simple woodcut prints.

A page from the Pauper's Bible

845 ▶ The **Vivian Bible**, one of the earliest illustrated Bibles, is commissioned by Count Vivian and produced in Tours, France in AD 845.

863 ▶ **Cyril and Methodius**, missionary brothers to Moravia (modern day Czech Republic), attempt to translate the Bible into Slavonic (AD 863). To do this, they develop an alphabet known as Glagolitic. Their alphabet later evolves into the Cyrillic alphabet used today throughout Eastern Europe and Russia.

The gospel of Mark in Glagolitic

1054 ▶ The **Great Schism** of 1054 becomes the final split between the Christian West (Roman Catholic Church) and the Christian East (Eastern Orthodox churches).

1066 ▶ The Normans from northern France conquer England in 1066. **Middle English** begins to develop from the mingling of Old English and French.

1200s ▶ In England, **Stephen Langton**, the Archbishop of Canterbury, divides the books of the Latin Vulgate Bible into chapters. These chapter divisions are still in use today.

Stephen Langton

1229 ▶ The **Inquisition** in France in 1229 forbids non-clergy from reading the Bible. The Papal Inquisition in Rome begins two years later.

1382 ▶ WYCLIFFE BIBLE

- A priest named John Wycliffe, later called "the Morning Star of the Reformation," teaches that Scripture, not church tradition, is the ultimate and final authority for God's people. His desire is for the people of England to have the Bible in their own language. Some church leaders strongly oppose this, believing that the Bible should only be read in "holy languages," like Latin.

John Wycliffe Reading His Translation of the Bible by Ford Madox Brown

- Undeterred, Wycliffe uses his influence to spur the translation of the Latin Vulgate into the English of his day. The first edition is completed in 1382. The "Wycliffe Bible" is the first complete English Bible.

- In the preface, Wycliffe's followers (ridiculed as Lollards, meaning "mumblers") include some of his criticisms of church traditions. The Wycliffe Bible is eventually banned and burned.

- Though Wycliffe dies of natural causes, those who oppose his views want to make sure he "died a heretic." So in 1428, more than forty years after his death, Wycliffe's bones are exhumed and burned for heresy.

1408 ▶ In **England** in 1408, it becomes illegal to translate or read the Bible in common English without the permission of a bishop.

1430 ▶ In 1430, Rabbi Moses Arragel translates the Old Testament into Castilian (Spanish). Today, it is known as the Bible of the House of Alba or the **Alba Bible**. The original is a work of art with beautiful illustrations and calligraphy.

1453 ▶ In 1453, Ottoman Turks capture the city of **Constantinople** (Istanbul today), the last holdout of the Eastern Empire. Scholars from Constantinople and the East migrate to Europe, bringing with them ancient Greek manuscripts of the New Testament. These manuscripts spur Western scholars to delve into the biblical languages and focus on original intent when interpreting the Scriptures.

Final assault and the fall of Constantinople
(Diorama in Askeri Museum, Istanbul, Turkey)

1456 ▸ THE PRINTING PRESS

Gutenberg Bible

- The world's first printing press with moveable metal type is invented in the mid-fifteenth century in Germany by Johann Gutenberg.
- In 1456, the Gutenberg Bible, an edition of the Latin Vulgate, is the first book printed on this printing press.
- This Bible is decorated and illuminated with hand painted letters and ornaments, bound in two volumes, and totals more than 1,200 pages.
- About two hundred copies of the Gutenberg Bible are printed. Today, only forty-seven copies survive.
- By the year 1500, Bibles reproduced on printing presses can be found all across Europe. Suddenly, the Bible is accessible to people who previously could not afford expensive handmade copies.

Printing press

1478 ▶ The **Spanish Inquisition** begins in 1478 and is carried out by both church and state authorities. Many translations of the Bible into common languages are put on the list of banned books.

1516 ▶ **Erasmus**, a priest and Greek scholar in the Dutch city of Rotterdam, publishes a Greek New Testament alongside a corrected Latin translation (1516). This text, known as *Novum Instrumentum Omne,* is the first published Greek New Testament. Later Greek editions based on Erasmus's work will be used by William Tyndale and the translators of the King James Version. In time, these Greek New Testaments become known in 1633 as *Textus Receptus*, meaning "Received Text."

The book of Revelation in Novum Instrumentum Omne

1522 ▶ The most influential person of the Protestant Reformation is a German monk named **Martin Luther**. He uses Erasmus's Greek text to translate the New Testament into German. He completes his translation in 1522 and his work helps standardize the German language.

Martin Luther

1526 ▶ WILLIAM TYNDALE

William Tyndale

- In 1526, William Tyndale, an Oxford scholar and priest, completes a translation of the New Testament into English working directly from the Greek texts.
- When Tyndale's bishop won't let him publish his work, he moves to Germany and prints his Bibles there, smuggling them back into England in sacks of corn and flour.
- Nine years later, he publishes part of the Old Testament translated from Hebrew.
- Executed by King Henry VIII for a litany of drummed up offenses (including producing a "corrupted" English Bible), Tyndale's final words are, "Lord, open the King of England's eyes."
- Tyndale's translation goes on to influence almost every later English translation of the Bible, earning Tyndale the name "Father of the English Bible."

1535 In 1535, the **Coverdale Bible** is completed by Miles Coverdale, a former monk and priest. This translation is based on Tyndale's work.

1537 The year after Tyndale's death, John Rogers, a clergyman and printer, publishes an English Bible under the pen name Thomas Matthew (1537). This Bible includes notes from past theologians and scholars like Augustine and Josephus, and becomes known as the **Matthew's Bible**. The initials "W. T." are printed between the Old and New Testaments as homage to William Tyndale. (Less than twenty years later, Rogers will be executed for refusing to renounce his Protestant beliefs.)

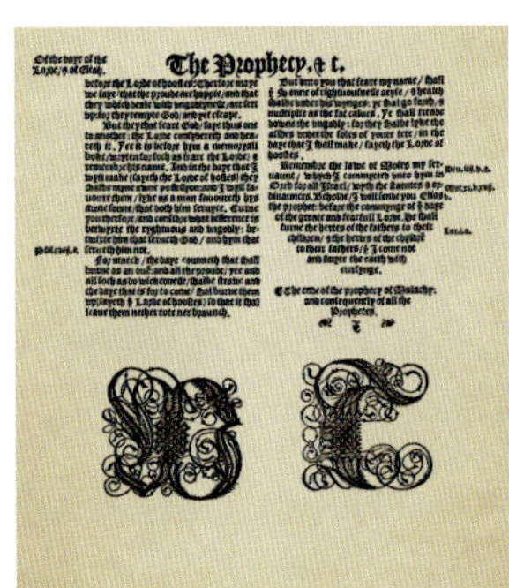
The Prophecy. &c.

Matthew's Bible
showing the initials W. T.

1539 Thomas Cromwell, advisor to King Henry VIII, authorizes Miles Coverdale to revise the Matthew's Bible. The result is the **Great Bible** (1539). A copy of this Bible is placed in every church in England by order of the archbishop Thomas Cranmer. To keep this Bible accessible to all people in the church, it is chained to the church pillars, so it also becomes known as the Chained Bible.

Council of Trent

1546 ▶ The Roman Catholic **Council of Trent** (1546) declares the Apocrypha to be Holy Scripture.

1551 ▶ In 1551, a scholar and printer named **Robert Stephanus** (a.k.a. Robert Estienne) separates the chapters of the Greek New Testament into verses. A few years later, the Geneva Bible becomes the first complete Bible with chapter and verse divisions that still exist today.

1553 ▶ **Queen Mary** ascends to the throne of England (1553). Mary swings the country back to Catholicism and bans Protestant translations of the English Bible. The Matthew's Bible translator John Rogers and the archbishop Thomas Cranmer are burned at the stake. Some three-hundred men, women, and children are also burned to death. This Protestant purge earns the queen the nickname "Bloody Mary."

Queen Mary

1560 ▶ THE GENEVA BIBLE

John Calvin

- In the wake of persecutions in England, many Protestant reformers flee to Switzerland and Germany.
- Some of these exiles in Switzerland publish the Geneva Bible (1560), which is a revision of the Great Bible with theological notes influenced by Protestant scholars, such as John Calvin, Theodore Beza, John Knox, and William Whittingham. Calvin writes the introduction.
- The Geneva Bible later becomes the Bible of William Shakespeare and John Bunyan, and also the Bible that the Pilgrims bring to America on the Mayflower.
- The 1640 edition of the Geneva Bible is the first English Bible to omit the Apocrypha completely. Earlier Protestant Bibles had included the Apocrypha in a separate section between the Old and New Testaments.

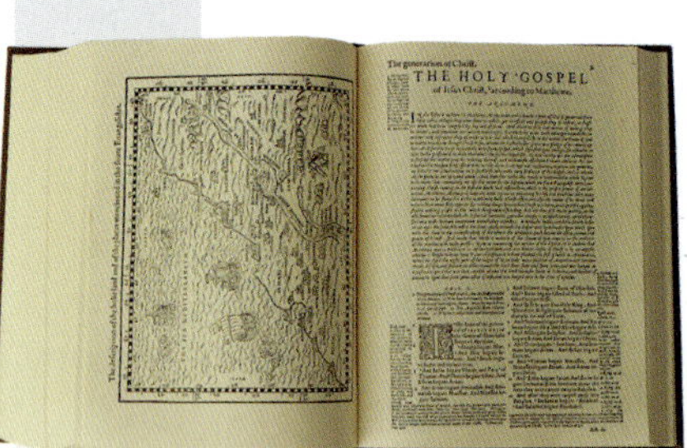

Geneva Bible

1568 ▸ Queen Mary dies in 1558, leaving the crown to Elizabeth, her younger half-sister. Elizabeth commissions a new English translation of the Bible which is completed in 1568. Because every bishop in the land is required to have a copy of this Bible, it becomes known as the **Bishop's Bible**. It never reaches the popularity of the Geneva Bible.

Bishop's Bible

1582 ▸ Exiled in France, the Catholic scholar Gregory Martin translates the New Testament into English in 1582. It is published in Rheims. He then completes and publishes the Old Testament in 1609 in Douai, France. Known as the **Douay-Rheims Bible**, Martin's work includes marginal notes that espouse Catholic teaching. This Bible becomes the standard English translation used by Roman Catholics for centuries.

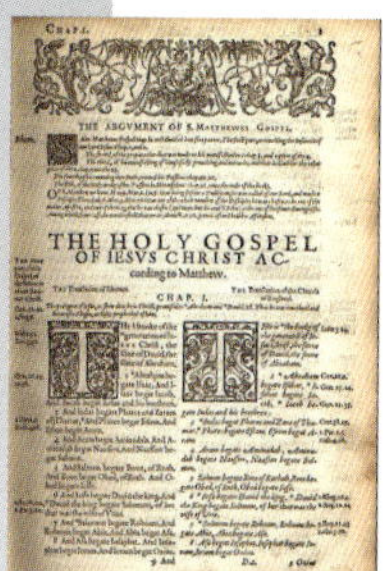
THE HOLY GOSPEL OF IESVS CHRIST AC-cording to Matthew.

Douay-Rheims Bible

1602 ▸ Protestant reformer Cipriano de Valera works for twenty years on a revision of a Spanish translation, the Reina Bible (1569). His revision comes to be known as **Reina-Valera** (1602). Today, this version is the most widely used Spanish Bible among Protestants.

1611 ▶ THE KING JAMES VERSION

King James Bible

- At a conference in 1604, Puritans ask King James to reform the Church of England. He agrees only to commission a new English translation of the Bible.
- Fifty-four scholars divided into six teams use earlier English translations, Greek New Testaments based on Erasmus's text, and various Hebrew and Aramaic texts. Their new version, known as the King James Version (or "Authorized Version") is completed in 1609 and published in 1611.
- This Bible is revised several times and becomes the most popular and influential English Bible for more than three hundred years.

King James

1620 ▶ In 1620, **Separatists** (Pilgrims), rejecting the Church of England, set sail to North America on the Mayflower, bringing with them the Geneva Bible.

1629 ▶ In 1629, the Orthodox Patriarch of Constantinople, as a gesture of peace, presents the earliest known copy of the Old and New Testaments in Greek to Charles I of England. This Bible is known as **Codex Alexandrinus** and dates to the fourth or fifth century. Western Bible translators finally have access to one of the earliest and most complete copies of the New Testament.

Codex Alexandrinus

1663 ▶ Puritan **John Eliot**, "the apostle to the Indians," translates the Bible into the language of Native Americans in Massachusetts (1663).

John Eliot preaching

1672 ▶ The Eastern Orthodox **Synod of Jerusalem** (1672) confirms the Apocrypha as genuine parts of Scripture.

1681 ▶ **João Ferreira d'Almeida** finishes the first Portuguese translation of the New Testament (1681).

1800s The **modern missionary movement** of the nineteenth century leads to a rapid increase in new Bible translations:

- **William Carey**, "the father of modern missions," translates the New Testament into Bengali (1801). Carey and his partners direct the translation of the Bible into more than forty Indian languages and dialects.
- Scottish missionary to China, **Robert Morrison**, translates the Bible into Chinese (1823).
- Native Cherokee speaker, **John Arch (Atsi)**, translates the gospel of John into Cherokee (1824). Cherokee pastor, **David Brown**, translates the New Testament one year later.
- **Karl Gutzlaff** translates portions of the Bible into Thai and Japanese (mid-1800s).
- A former slave from Yoruba (modern Nigeria), **Samuel Ajayi Crowther**, translates parts of the New Testament into his native language of Yoruba (1852).

Bishop Samuel Ajayi Crowther

- **Robert Moffat**, a Scottish missionary to Africa, translates the Bible into the African language of Tswana (1857).

1859 In the mid-nineteenth century, the earliest known complete copy of the Greek New Testament is found at St. Catherine's Monastery near Mount Sinai, Egypt. Carefully copied and corrected, **Codex Sinaiticus**, which dates to the fourth century, is one of the oldest and most reliable surviving complete manuscripts of the New Testament.

St. Catherine's Monastery

1860s **Codex Vaticanus**, a near-complete copy of the Greek Old and New Testaments dating to the fourth century, is made available to scholars in the 1800s. It is believed to be slightly older than Codex Sinaiticus. It had been stored in the Vatican Library since at least the fifteenth century (possibly longer)—and it is still there today.

Codex Vaticanus

1881 Named after its editors, Brooke Foss Westcott and Fenton John Anthony Hort, the **Westcott-Hort Greek New Testament** (1881) becomes the standard Greek text until 1945. It serves as the foundation for many English New Testament translations, such as the Revised Version and the American Standard Version.

1885 ▶ Scholars in England revise the King James Version to reflect the findings from manuscripts discovered during the two previous centuries. Their goal is to work from more reliable Greek, Hebrew, and Aramaic texts, and to retranslate words based on new linguistic information about these ancient languages. This translation becomes known as the **English Revised Version** (1885). The American Standard Version (1901) is the American edition of the English Revised Version.

1924 ▶ Universal Braille Press (later Braille Institute of America) publishes the first complete **Braille Bible** (1924). The Braille Bible in the King James Version consists of twenty-one volumes.

Braille Bible

1920s ▶ In the 1920s, excavations in the ancient city of Ugarit (in northern Syria today) lead to the discovery of a previously unknown language. **Ugaritic** is an ancient Semitic language similar to Hebrew. This discovery helps scholars better understand Hebrew vocabulary in the Old Testament.

List of gods in Ugaritic

1935 During the twentieth century, more than a hundred New Testament manuscripts are found in Egypt. Among them is the **John Rylands Fragment P52** (identified in 1935), which is the oldest surviving fragment of the New Testament, dating to the early second century. This papyrus is a fragment of John 18:31–33, 37–38, the chapter in which Jesus stands trial before Pilate.

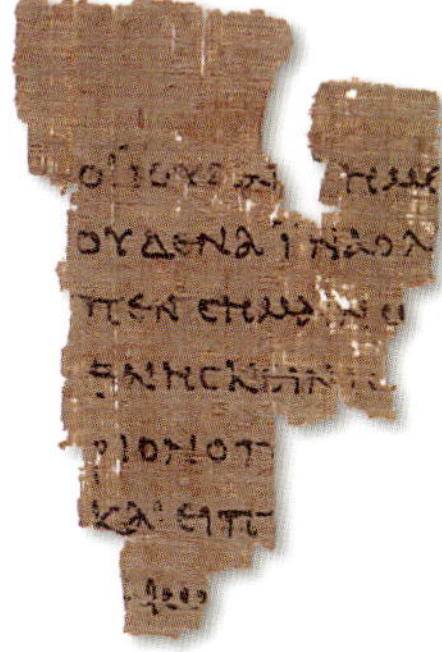

P52 (John Rylands Papyrus Greek 457)

1946 A treasure trove of scrolls are discovered in caves along the Dead Sea (1946–1948). These are some of the oldest known copies of portions of the Old Testament. Scholars date these copies to between 300 BC and AD 40. A scroll of Isaiah from these **Dead Sea Scrolls** is the oldest complete manuscript of any book of the Bible copied before the time of Christ. The scrolls provide confirmation that the methods used to preserve the Masoretic Text were effective.

Ancient jars in Qumran

1950s In the 1950s, Kurt Aland edits the 1898 Greek New Testament by German scholar Eberhard Nestle. This edited version becomes known as **Nestle-Aland Novum Testamentum Graece**. To date, there have been twenty-eight editions which form the foundation of many modern translations, such as the English Standard Version, the New American Standard Bible, and the New International Version.

Nestle-Aland Novum Testamentum Graece

1965 The **Amplified Bible** is translated by Frances E. Siewert and twelve others and published in 1965. This Bible has a unique system of punctuation, typefaces, and synonyms in parentheses to more fully explain words in the Bible. For example, John 3:16 reads, "For God so greatly loved and dearly prized the world that He [even] gave up His only begotten (unique) Son, so that whoever believes in (trusts in, clings to, relies on) Him shall not perish (come to destruction, be lost) but have eternal (everlasting) life."

Amplified Bible

1966 In 1966, the **Jerusalem Bible** (now called the New Jerusalem Bible) is completed, having been commissioned in response to Pope Pius XII's request for a more clear, skilled translation by Dominicans and others at Ecole Biblique in Jerusalem. J. R. R. Tolkien, author of *The Lord of the Rings*, was one of the contributing translators.

Pope Pius XII

1971 The **New American Standard Bible** (1971) is published by the Lockman Foundation. This Bible seeks to remove antiquated English phrases and words and add modern punctuation.

1978 The first edition of the **New International Version** is published in 1978. The most recent revision (2011) brings the translation into line with shifts in the English language, and also uses a more inclusive language (gender neutral pronouns if the terms do not specify a gender). This Bible is currently the best-selling English version.

New International Version

1979 ▶ The film ***Jesus***, a cinematic version of the gospel of Luke, is released in 1979. Spearheaded by Campus Crusade for Christ (now known as Cru), this evangelistic film will, over its first forty years of release, be translated into some 1,800 languages and shown to more than a billion people.

1982 ▶ In 1982, a modern language translation that seeks to maintain the structure and beauty of the King James Version is published. It's called (fittingly) the **New King James Version**.

1996 ▶ The **New International Reader's Version** (1996) becomes the translation with the lowest reading level of any major English Bible. It is used by children and adults for whom English is not their first language.

1996 ▶ The **New Living Translation** is published in 1996 to provide an easy-to-read modern version. This translation removes theological terms and instead uses the definition. For example, the term *justification* is replaced with "made right with God."

New Living Translation

1999 ▶ The **Nueva Version Internacional**, a Spanish translation directly from the Hebrew and Greek texts, is published in 1999. This Bible is the second most-popular Spanish translation used today. (Its English counterpart is the New International Version.)

Nueva Version Internacional

2001 ▶ The **English Standard Version** is completed in 2001 with over a hundred translators. It is a theologically conservative translation and typically avoids inclusive language.

2002 ▶ Eugene Peterson publishes his paraphrase version of the Bible called **The Message** (2002). This version re-creates the common language in which the Bible was written into today's common language in English. For example, John 3:16 reads, "This is how much God loved the world: He gave his Son, his one and only Son. And this is why: so that no one need be destroyed; by believing in him, anyone can have a whole and lasting life."

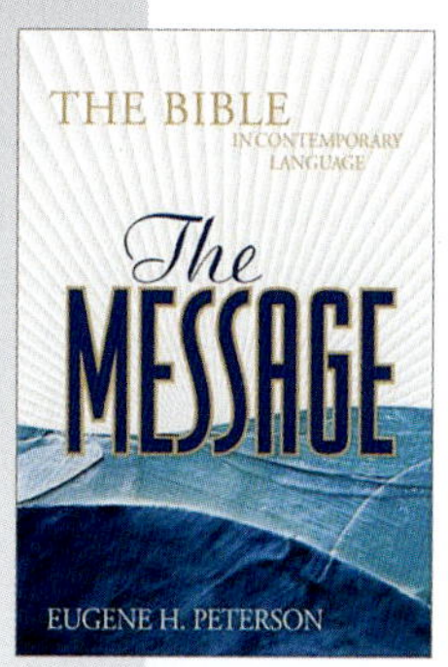

The Message

2004 ▶ The **Holman Christian Standard Bible** (today called the Christian Standard Bible) is published in 2004 and sponsored by LifeWay Christian Resources of the Southern Baptist Convention and Holman Bible Publishers. This translation uses unique renderings for the names of God: Lord (Adonai), God (Elohim), LORD (YHWH), God Almighty (El Shaddai), etc.

Holman Christian Standard Bible

2008 ▶ YouVersion launches the **Bible App**® (2008), providing a way for people to read the Bible on their phones. Today, this app offers the Bible in more than 1,350 languages.

2011 ▶ **New American Bible Revised Edition** is an English Catholic version published in 2011. It's a revision of the New American Bible (1970). This Bible includes the Apocrypha and is approved by the US Conference of Catholic Bishops for personal study, devotion, Mass, and liturgy.

New American Bible Revised Edition

2011 The **Common English Bible** (2011) is completed by more than a hundred translators from twenty-two faith traditions in American, African, Asian, European, and Latino communities. Its goal is to be a translation accessible to a broad range of English speakers.

Common English Bible

2019 In 2019, more than **93 million Bibles** are printed. About 27% of people own at least one full printed Bible, and 66% of the world's population can access a full Bible in their own language on the internet.[10]

2019 **Wycliffe Global Alliance** estimates that as of 2019, some 3,384 languages have at least a portion of the Bible, and 1,548 languages have a full New Testament or more. There are nearly 6,500 languages spoken worldwide today.[11]

2020 In the twenty-first century, shifts in **Christian populations** continue, with twice as many Christians living in the Global South (Africa, Asia, Latin America, and Oceania) than in the Global North (Europe and North America). Spanish becomes the language most spoken by Christians, followed next by English, Portuguese, Russian, and Mandarin Chinese.[12]

NOW WHAT?

How to Get the Most out of Your Bible Reading

IT'S GREAT TO KNOW HOW WE GOT THE BIBLE. But it's even better to know how to get *into* the Bible—and how to get its life-changing truth into our hearts.

Here's the good news about getting into God's Word: You don't have to know Greek and Hebrew or learn Aramaic or be an expert in theology. Just grab a Bible and start reading. You can install a Bible app on your phone or get an audio Bible and start listening.

Five Tips for Bible Reading

1. **READ PRAYERFULLY.** Ask God to give you "ears to hear" what he wants to say to you. Pray the prayer of the psalmist: *"Open my eyes that I may see wonderful things in your law"* (Psalm 119:18).

2. **READ ATTENTIVELY.** Stop multitasking when you open the Bible. Give God's Word your full attention. Be like an observant detective and notice all that you can.

3. **READ HUMBLY.** Don't merely read the Bible; let it read *you*. Let it be a like a mirror, showing you where you need to grow and change. James 1:21 urges, "*Humbly accept the word God has planted in your hearts, for it has the power to save your souls.*"

4. **READ DAILY.** In truth, God's Word is spiritual food for our souls. In the same way that you would be weak if you only ate one or two meals a week, you need divine truth every day.

5. **READ EXPECTANTLY.** Someone has pointed out that God didn't give us his Word to make us smarter sinners, but to make us holier saints. Cheesy? Maybe, but it's also true. God's truth has the power to change us . . . *if we let it*. Read it, believing that God is able to make you holy with his truth. As Jesus prayed for his followers, "*Sanctify them by the truth; your word is truth*" (John 17:17).

QUESTIONS FOR DISCUSSION

1. If you did a survey and asked a hundred neighbors, classmates, coworkers, etc., to say the first thing that comes to mind when they hear the word *Bible*, what responses do you think you would get? What response would you give if you were asked?

2. What are some criticisms you most often hear about the Bible? Which of these do you think are exaggerated? Which ones bother you the most?

3. What is your own "history" with the Bible? For example, do you own a Bible? When did you get it and why? What translation is it? Have you ever read the entire Bible cover to cover? If so, what was that experience like? If not, what do you think keeps you from reading the whole Bible?

4. Do any books (or sections) in the Bible make you wonder, *How did this make it into God's Word?* Why do you think that's your reaction?

5. Read 2 Peter 1:16–21. In your own words, how would you explain what the apostle Peter is saying? How would you summarize it?

6. Do archaeological discoveries like the Dead Sea Scrolls strengthen your faith? Or do they make no difference to your faith? Why?

7. It's been suggested that it might actually be a bad thing if we had the original biblical writings—for example, the actual stone tablets that God gave Moses on Sinai or the apostle Paul's letter to the Romans—because such things would likely become objects of worship. Do you agree? Why or why not?

8. Throughout history—and also in some places in the world today—attempts have been made to ban, eradicate, or in some way withhold the Bible from people. Why do you think there is such animosity toward Scripture? What does it mean to you that ultimately all these efforts have been unsuccessful?

9. What is something you learned from this overview of how we got the Bible? What stood out to you most in the time line of the history of the Bible?

10. What topic in this study do you want to explore more fully? What questions do you still have?

Notes

1 Cited in Norman L. Geisler and William E. Nix, *A General Introduction to the Bible* (Chicago: Moody Press, 1986), 475.

2 Wycliffe Global Alliance http://www.wycliffe.net/en/statistics (December 16, 2019).

3 Cited in Guinness World Records https://www.guinnessworldrecords.com/world-records/best-selling-book-of-non-fiction/ (December 16, 2019).

4 The Bible App® https://www.youversion.com/the-bible-app/ (January 24, 2020).

5 World Christian Database (Leiden: Brill) cited in *World Christianity* (Peabody, MA: Rose Publishing, 2020).

6 Eric Ray, *Sofer: The Story of a Torah Scroll* (Lewisville, NC: Torah Aura Productions, 1998), 17.

7 *The Confession of Dositheus* (Synod of Jerusalem, 1672) [Question 3].

8 Timothy Paul Jones, *How We Got the Bible* (Carson, CA: Rose Publishing, 2015) 78.

9 Timothy Paul Jones, *How We Got the Bible* (Carson, CA: Rose Publishing, 2015) 94.

10 World Christian Database (Leiden: Brill) cited in *World Christianity* (Peabody, MA: Rose Publishing, 2020).

11 Wycliffe Global Alliance http://www.wycliffe.net/en/statistics (December 16, 2019).

12 World Christian Database (Leiden: Brill) cited in *World Christianity* (Peabody, MA: Rose Publishing, 2020).

Image Credits

Images used under license from Shutterstock.com: Cover image FotoDuets; Page 9 Elzbieta Sekowska; 10 Jjustas; 12 James Steidl; 13 Amanda Carden; 14 Marco Ossino; 17 Cris Foto; 21 Lerner Vadim; 24 Awe Inspiring Images; 27 Andrey_Popov; 28 jsp; 34 airphoto.gr; 39 Bakusova; 40 ChameleonsEye; 42 Samuel Perry; 44 Renata Sedmakova; 47 Renata Sedmakova; 52 DyziO; 53 Nathan Holland; 54 Timothy R. Nichols; 62 Morphart Creation; 66 steve estvanik; 67 Dja65; 68 dugdax; 72 Georgios Kollidas; 74 Everett Historical; 76 Take Photo; 77 eFesenko; 78 Karin Hildebrand Lau; 79 photoshooter2015; 80 Madeleine R; 81 Yaroslaff.

Other images: Page 30 "A Sofer (Jewish scribe) completing the Book of Esther, Ein Bokek, Israel, January 2012" Wikimedia Commons, Spaceboyjosh; 41 Jar and Cover for Manuscript rolls, Walters Art Museum; 43 Jesus Unrolls the Book in the Synagogue, Brooklyn Museum; 58 Marble portrait head of Emperor Constantine, Metropolitan Museum of Art; 59 Saint Jerome in His Study, Walters Art Museum; 61 Sculpture of St. Augustine of Canterbury, Canterbury Cathedral, Wikimedia Commons, Saforrest; 64 Plaster maquette of Stephen Langton, Wikimedia Commons, Linda Spashett Storye book; 67 Gutenberg Bible, Flickr, JMWK; 71 Council of Trent, Wikimedia Commons, Laurom; 72 Geneva Bible, Wikimedia Commons, Hi540; 78 Ugaritic tablet, Wikimedia Commons, Rama, Louvre Museum.